ANIMALS IN DANGER

ORANGUTANS

By Emily Kington

Words that appear in **BOLD** are explained in the glossary.

First published by
Hungry Tomato Ltd in 2022
F1, Old Bakery Studios,
Blewetts Wharf, Malpas Road,
Truro, Cornwall, TR1 1QH, UK.

www.hungrytomato.com

ISBN 978-1-914087-59-2

A CIP catalog record for this book is available from the British Library.

Manufactured in the USA.

Picture Credits (t=top, b=bottom, m=middle, l-left, r=right, bg= background)

Digital Vision: 1bg, 9br, 30ml, 26bl, 27bl. **Alamy:** 17tr, 24bl, 25ml, 25mr, 25tr. **Superstock:** 25bl. Orangutan Foundartion UK: 27mr. **Shutterstock:** Ares Jonekson 29tl; Arief Budi Kusuma 18-19bg; Christian Edelmann 13br; DH Saragih 28tr; Erika J Mitchell 30br; Jackal Yu 26mr; Kristina Ismulyani 20-21bg; L-N 29b, 32br; Longjourneys 10-11bg; Lukaszemanphoto 2bg; Lukaszemanphoto 3bg, 22-23bg; Lukaszemanphoto 4-5bg; Magic Orb Studio 18tl; Maksim Safaniuk 12-13bg; Marie Martin 14-15bg; Mark Nazh 28br; Open Mind Art 27t; Paramarta Bari 29tr; REC Stock Footage 31bg, 6-7bg, 30br; Salvacampillo 8-9bg; Sergey uryadnikov 21br; Thammanoon Khamchalee 28bl; Torsten Pursche 10bl; Tristan tan 16-17bg.

Every effort has been made to trace the copyright holders, and we apologize in advance for any unintentional omissions. We would be pleased to insert the appropriate acknowledgements in any subsequent edition of this publication.

CONTENTS

THE WORLD OF THE ORANGUTAN

Orangutans are large tree-living apes. They live in rainforests on the islands of Sumatra and Borneo in South East Asia.

For years, people thought there were only two types of orangutan, Bornean orangutans and Sumatran orangutans. In 2017, a new species was confirmed, the Tapanuli orangutan.

DID YOU KNOW?

Baby Orangutans stay with their mothers for up to seven years.

ADULT ORANGUTANS

Adult orangutans live alone. Each orangutan has its own territory in the rainforest.

Males and females only meet for mating.

Male orangutans often fight if another male comes near.

Male orangutans look quite different from females. They are nearly twice as big, and have large cheek pouches at the sides of their faces.

DID YOU KNOW?

A big male orangutan's arms can span 7.5 feet (2.3 m).

THE HUNT FOR FOOD

DID YOU KNOW?

For the first few months, baby orangutans only drink their mom's milk. Later, they eat fruit, which is chewed and softened for them by their mom.

Orangutans need to travel long distances through the rainforest to find their food.

They mostly travel above the ground, using their powerful arms to swing from one branch to another.

Orangutans eat many different sorts of food, such as fruit and leaves, birds' eggs, snails and **termites**.

At night, the rainforest is full of the sounds of insects and nocturnal creatures.

Orangutans build sleeping nests high up in the forks of trees.

These nests are made by bending branches into a bowl shape. The orangutans fill the bowl with leaves to make it soft and snug.

Orangutan in his nest.

NIGHT IN THE FOREST

RAINFOREST IN DANGER

DID YOU KNOW?

Trees are cut down to be made into paper and to make room for goldmines and farmland.

The biggest threat facing the orangutan is the destruction of the rainforest.

The islands where orangutans live are crowded with people. Many of these people are poor. Cutting timber from the forest is often the only way they can earn enough to live.

In some places there are laws to protect the forest, but because there are not enough people to enforce the laws, the **logging** is not stopped.

POACHERS

Some people kill or capture orangutans. This is called poaching.

In the past, some orangutans were killed for food. Now the poaching problem has become much worse because many people want baby orangutans for pets.

The poachers treat the orangutans very cruelly. Often the mom is killed to make it easier to take the baby.

ORANGUTANS FOR SALE

Baby orangutans can be sold for a lot of money. But this does not mean that they are well looked after by the poachers.

They are often put into tiny cages and sold at markets by the side of the road. Sometimes they are not fed properly.

DID YOU KNOW?

Out of every ten babies captured, eight or nine will die before they reach their new owner.

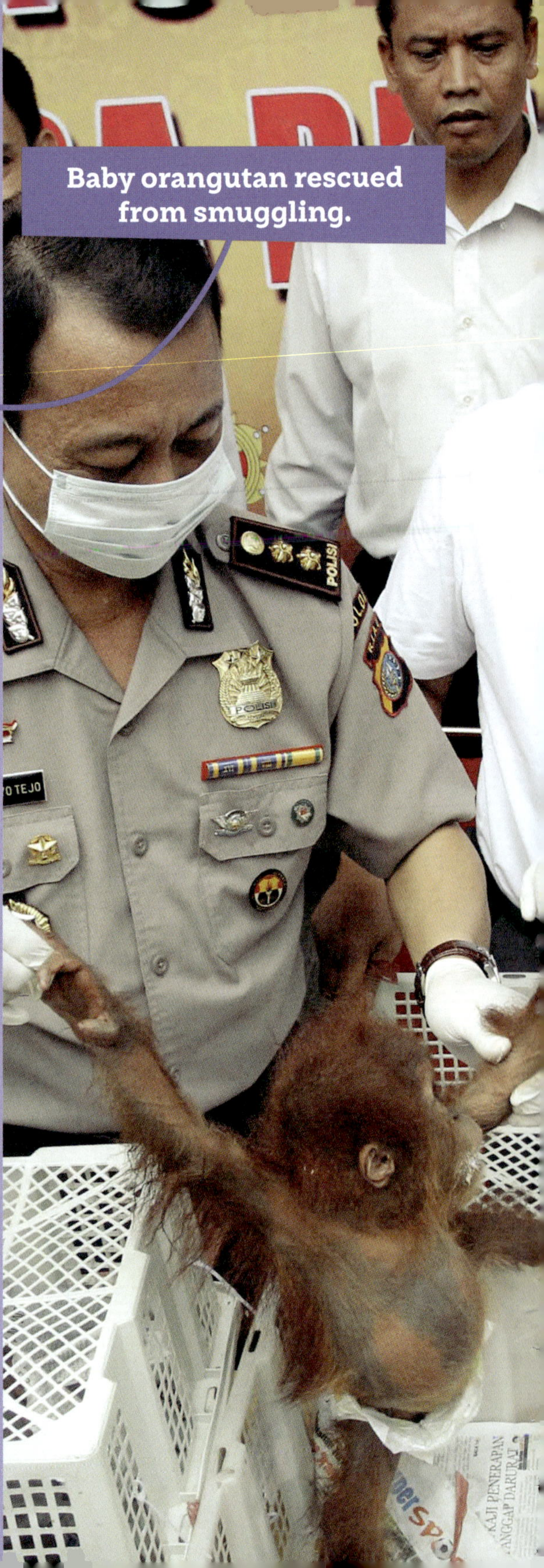

Baby orangutan rescued from smuggling.

Orangutans do not make good pets. When they become adults, they are very strong and can be bad tempered.

When people get tired of their pet orangutans, many of the animals are killed.

The lucky ones might go to a rescue center. Here they are looked after until they are ready to live by themselves, back in the rainforest.

At rescue centers, vets check the orangutans to make sure they have not picked up a disease while they have been living with humans.

RESCUE CENTERS

BORN TO BE WILD

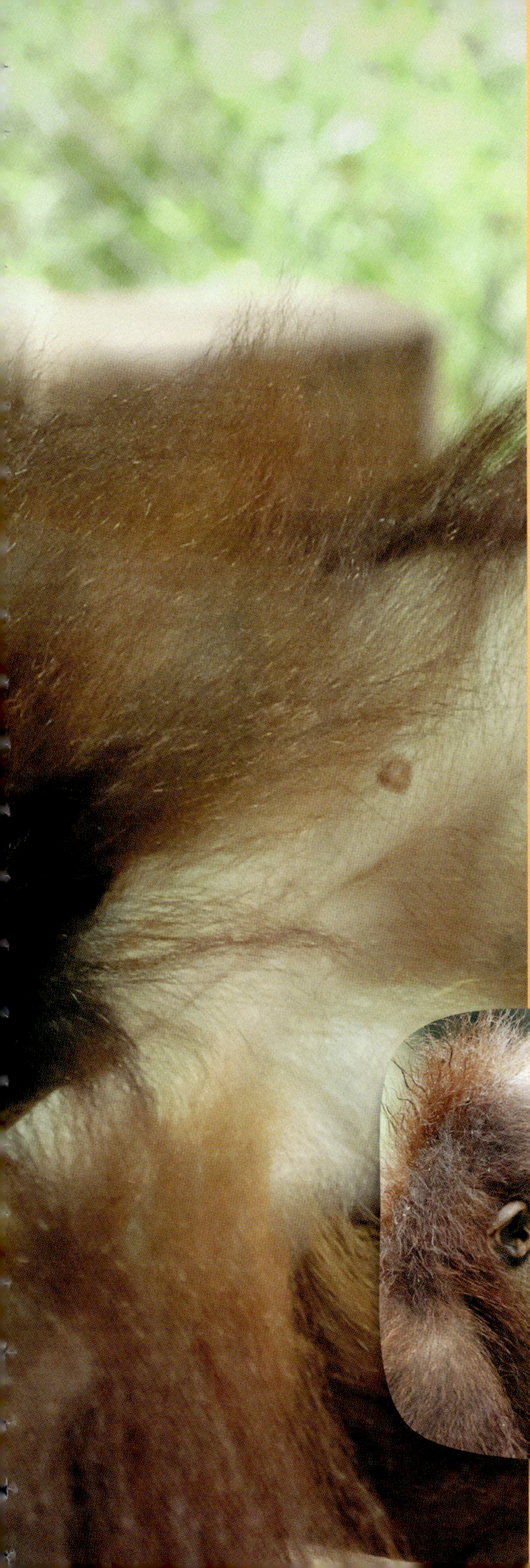

In the wild, young orangutans learn what food is safe to eat, and where to find it. They also learn how to travel through the rainforest and how to stay safe.

Babies that have been kept as pets do not know how to do these things.

The rescue center carers start to teach the babies by putting food on feeding platforms up in the rainforest trees.

Slowly, the young orangutans will learn where to find their own food.

PROTECTING THE ORANGUTANS

The rescued orangutans are released into nature reserves.

Forest rangers patrol the reserves and loggers and poachers are not allowed into these areas.

But there are still problems. Governments of the countries where orangutans live can't afford to pay for enough rangers to make sure that the animals are safe.

Outside the reserves, orangutans are not protected at all, and their **habitat** is disappearing fast.

DID YOU KNOW?

Unless a lot more is done to protect them, scientists say that orangutans could become **extinct** in the wild in just ten years.

FACT FILE

WHERE DO ORANGUTANS LIVE?

Orangutans are found on the islands of Sumatra and Borneo in South East Asia.

- They now only live in the places shown in red on the main map.

- Orangutans live high in the rainforest trees, about 100 feet (30 m) above the ground.

DID YOU KNOW?

The name orangutan means 'person of the forest' in the Malay language.

ORANGUTANS BODIES

Orangutans are the largest tree-living animals in the world.

- Their red fur is perfect **camouflage** in the rainforest. They are almost impossible to spot from the ground.

An adult male orangutan has leathery cheek pouches.

Female
Height: up to 3.3 ft
Weight: 110 lbs

Male
Height: up to 4.6 ft
Weight: 299 lbs

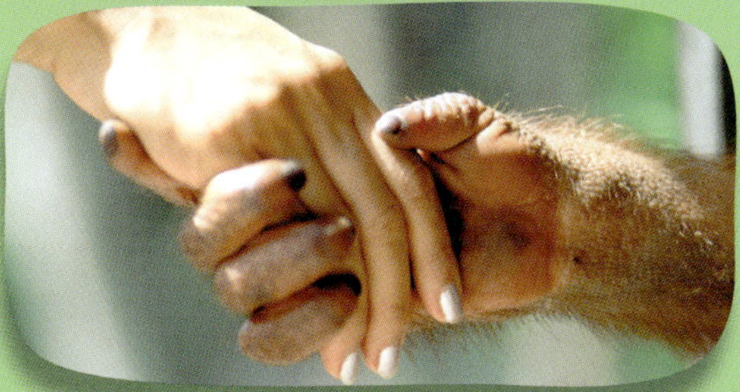

- Orangutans have very similar hands to humans.

FACT FILE

ORANGUTANS IN DANGER

Orangutans are all in danger of extinction. There are fewer than 800 Tapanuli orangutans left in the wild, making them the rarest of the great apes.

- In recent years, over 80% of the rainforest where orangutans live has been cut down or destroyed by fires.

- The small areas left are not big enough to support large numbers of orangutans.

- Some orangutans are killed for food. This is known as 'bush meat'

- Poachers take baby orangutans from their mom's to sell as pets. Often the mom is killed.

FACT FILE

CONSERVATION

Conservationists are working hard to protect orangutans and their habitat. Here are some of the things they are doing:

- Planting trees to try to recover forest that has been lost, so that wildlife can return.

- Working hard to prevent more rainforest from being cut down.

- Rescuing orangutans that have been poached and reintroducing them back into the wild.
- Fighting forest fires.

HOW YOU CAN HELP

There are some great animal conservation charities and wildlife reserves that need money to pay for the work that they do. There are lots of fun ways that you could help to raise money and awareness for them.

- Why not organize a tasty bake sale?
- Ask people to sponsor you to do an activity. This could be something like a walk or a run, or helping to pick up trash in your local area.
- Put on a community or school event. How about a disco or a charity run?

Don't forget to get your family, friends and teachers involved! It'll be easier and much more fun with some help!

GLOSSARY

apes A group of mammals that includes orangutans, chimpanzees, gorillas and humans.

camouflage Fur or skin that makes an animal hard to see in the place where it lives.

conservationists People who take care of the natural world. Conservationists try to stop people hunting endangered animals and they ask governments to pass laws to protect wild habitats.

extinct When a type of animal or plant completely disappears.

forest rangers People whose job it is to look after protected nature reserves and the animals that live there. They work for governments and sometimes for conservation organizations.

habitat The place that suits a particular animal or plant in the wild.

logging Cutting down trees for wood.

nature reserves Protected areas where the killing of animals or the cutting down of trees is against the law.

nocturnal When an animal is only active at night.

poaching The capturing or killing of animals by poachers so that they, or parts of their bodies, can be sold.

rainforests Warm, wet places where lots of trees and plants grow. Many animals, such as monkeys, gibbons and clouded leopards, live in the rainforests where the orangutans live.

termites Insects a bit like ants that live in large groups.

territory The area in which an animal or a family of animals lives.

INDEX